THE NEW YOU

The New You is ideal to keep around as a resource aid . . . something to leave on your dresser to pick up when questions come . . . and to read when you need insights into how God's Word can get into your life *today*. Read through it at a pace comfortable to you, then keep it around. It can be a starter toward making you genuinely new through Christ and His Word, the Bible.

THE NEW YOU

Straight answers to tough questions for new Christians

HAROLD MYRA

VICTOR BOOKS

a division of SP Publications, Inc.
WHEATON, ILLINOIS 60187

Offices also in Fullerton, California • Whitby, Ontario, Canada • Amersham-on-the-Hill, Bucks, England

Written by Harold Myra. Concepts and illustrations from various sources, including: Larry Anderson, Bruce Barton, Clayton Baumann, Jim Green, Ron Hutchcraft, Jay Kesler, Dean Merrill, Ken Overstreet, Dave Veerman; books by Stephen W. Brown, C. S. Lewis, Paul Little, J. B. Phillips, Francis Schaeffer, David Winter, and others. Scripture quotations from *The Living Bible,* © 1971 by Tyndale House. Used by permission.

Third printing, 1981

Introduction

For years we have struggled with the problem of developing materials which would help kids truly understand what happens to them when they receive Christ—and how they can grow in Him and develop an understanding of God's Word.

The usual attempt to boil all Christian truth into a booklet and expect a new Christian to absorb it simply bewilders.

I am convinced that Jesus certainly had the right idea when He used parables and various illustrations to make spiritual truth understandable. The strange thing is, Christians have often gone the opposite way and taken out all the story part for the new Christians. Follow-up materials often try to make them instant theologians by the end of a short booklet.

The New You fits both new Christians and kids who have known the Lord for some time and want to grow in their Christian lives. We've included extensive biblical truth, but we've also worked to make it understandable. The present format of questions and answers—based on research into the actual questions of thousands of new Christians—is usable as a read-through paperback or as a discussion book for groups or one-to-one interaction.

Welcome!

You've become a follower of Jesus Christ? That's Good News! In fact, it's the most important thing that's ever happened to you.

You're probably wondering, though, just what it all means. What happened to you? How is it supposed to affect you? How is *He* supposed to affect you?

Here's what the Bible says about the New You:

What God Did for You

"For God loved the world so much that He gave His only Son so that anyone who believes in Him shall not perish but have eternal life."

—John 3:16

What You Did

"But to all who received Him, He gave the right to become children of God. All they needed to do was to trust Him to save them."

—John 1:11, 12

The New You

"When someone becomes a Christian he becomes a brand new person inside. He is not the same any more. A new life has begun!"

—2 Corinthians 5:17

What You Have Now

". . . You have everything when you have Christ, and you are filled with God through your union with Christ. He is the highest ruler, with authority over every other power."

—Colossians 2:9, 10

Where You Fit In

"For His Holy Spirit speaks to us deep in our hearts, and tells us that we really are God's children."

—Romans 8:16

Now You Can Face God

"And as we live with Christ, our love grows more perfect and complete; so we will not be ashamed and embarrassed at the day of judgment, but can face Him with confidence and joy, because He loves us and we love Him too."

—1 John 4:17

THE
NEW YOU

1 *I accepted Christ three weeks ago, but already I feel like I'm a poor excuse for a Christian. Other kids are so much more devoted to Christ than I am. It makes me kinda depressed.*

Your attitude — although it depresses you now — will help you over the long range. Why? Because instead of feeling secure and "with it" spiritually, you realize how far you have to go.

Perhaps you wouldn't be nearly so depressed if you knew how much the other kids struggle. Some are fighting deep problems. Others may actually be superficial under all their spiritual gianthood.

Long
way
to go

A senior was with about 200 kids, jammed into a motel lobby at a youth group retreat. They were praying God would reach into their lives, clean them up, give them power. The senior was deeply touched by God, his face actually wet with tears. He saw his utter selfishness.

He also saw a girl he knew well get up to counsel other kids — and he felt just like you do. "Wow. She must really be up spiritually. I'm empty without God. I fail Him so much!"

Yet it was the guy who went on to a deeper faith and a full-time ministry for Christ. The girl eventually chucked the whole thing.

The point is not the girl's problem, whatever it was, but the guy's attitude which led to wholeness. His saying, "God be merciful to me a sinner," with genuine tears, enabled him to grow and grow and grow. [1]

That's what it's all about — you're starting a lifetime of growth. It's not nearly so important where you are now as what direction you're going. And how spiritually hungry you are. Are you open for Christ to begin a growth program that will continue on and on?

Your growth is based on a whole new relationship. John 1:12 says, "But to all who received Him (Jesus), He gave the right to become children of God." You're a newly-born member of God's family. You have a new heavenly Father — a Father who is perfect.

Birth is only the beginning.

Let's take this whole Bible idea of our being new-born and talk about it awhile. A baby comes noisily into the world and can cause lots of commotion — but actually, he's very limited. He doesn't exactly hop off the delivery table, slip on some jeans and trot downstairs to hail a taxi. In the same way, spiritual birth is just a beginning. There are years of growth ahead.

[1] See Luke 18:9-14.

It's absurd to think of a baby hopping off the delivery table. It's equally absurd to envision staying a day-old baby for months. Eventually, lying there in the post-delivery room, he'd begin thinking, "Man, I don't enjoy being a human at all. There's nothing to it! I got slapped around a couple of times by this guy. I can't breathe too well, and they've got me in a hot little box. Here I lie, farsighted, red-faced."

Obviously that's impossible. But you can stay in the baby stage spiritually — to remain on the delivery table and miss out on growing as a Christian and seeing all the great things God wants to do in you. Second Peter 3:18 says, "Grow in grace and in the knowledge of our Lord and Saviour Jesus Christ." Colossians 2:6 and 7 sums it up: "And now just as you trusted Christ to save you, trust Him, too, for each day's problems; live in vital union with Him. Let your roots grow down into Him and draw up nourishment from Him. See that you go on growing in the Lord, and become strong and vigorous in the truth."

And all that takes time. If you've ever taken care of a baby, you know it takes awhile for it to catch onto things. The first few months babies just lie there like blobs, except when they're crying for food or a dry diaper. You can make faces, wrinkle your nose and chin, gurgle — but no response.

For the first year or so, the kid can't even burp by himself.

He starts discovering his fingers. He starts looking at faces. He rolls over, then crawls and finally walks. He says, "Gagagale bagaga" which his father insists is "Da da."

As he's learning all this, can you imagine a father — as baby starts to talk — slugging him and saying, "You stupid kid, say it right! Don't say it till you can say it right!" When baby starts to crawl and drops awkwardly on his rear, a father wouldn't say,

"I don't want to see you try *that* again! Do it right the first time, or don't do it at all!" No, a father is delighted with any progress. Growth is a slow, but sure, process.

In the same way, our Father is interested in our growth, though we may stumble and mess up. God's there to help us, not put us down.

A baby also learns there are "no-nos" in life. Right things to do and wrong things. A bottle on the table will break if tipped over. Mustn't touch! A small child finds that if he's going to get along in life, it's best to get along with Father. And the way to do that is to see things *his* way.

Our heavenly Father — unlike human fathers — is always right. When we do wrong things, the way to restore fellowship is to see it His way. To apologize. And to obey the next time. First John 1:9 says, " . . . if we confess our sins to Him, He can be depended on to forgive us and to cleanse us from every wrong."

When you were born into God's family, He accepted you with love as if you were perfect. Hebrews 10:14 tells us, "For by that one offering He made forever perfect in the sight of God all those whom He is making holy."

That's you! Perfect. And beloved. Notice the growth factor — "is *making* holy." Philippians 1:6 says, " . . . God who began the good work within you will keep right on helping you grow in His grace until His task within you is finally finished. . . ."

Don't worry about others being more devoted. Just look at the exciting things your Father wants to do in *you!*

2 *When I said to Jesus, "Come on in. You've got me" — when I finally said that after fighting Him for a long time — I was really close to Him. I mean, I could feel it. He was there. But now, I don't always feel that way anymore. I do sometimes, but just as often I can't tell that I'm any different or that He's around. In fact, sometimes I feel rotten. Was it all a farce? Have I lost Christ?*

Consider what God has said: "I will never, never fail you nor forsake you."[1]

He doesn't say, "If you feel I'm close, I'll not forsake you." No — He states a fact. You were born into God's family. That's not based on feelings any more than the law of gravity. It's based on God's promise to you.

Most people go through a case of the blahs some time after their conversion. But if you genuinely received Christ, His promise is not void. Birth is forever. The relationship doesn't change: your Father is still your Father.

That doesn't mean, of course, that *communication* can't break down. You can be on the outs with your dad, for instance, because you wracked up his car. But he's still your dad. You just have to repair the communication break (and, perhaps, the car).

We must get three things in the right order: *Facts, Faith* and *Feeling. Facts* must be first. They're most important. They're based on God and His Word. Then comes *Faith* — our belief in those *Facts.* Our

[1] Hebrews 3:15.

15

At first your feelings may run high.
But even though your emotions can go from
rock bottom to mountaintop, you can
hang onto something solid.

Time for a new dad?

Feelings of joy and assurance come last. Not that *Feelings* aren't a great fringe benefit to the Christian life and one God often gives us. But it has to be third in line. If we allow our *Faith* to turn around and march backward while looking at *Feelings*, we'll stumble. *Feelings* are nice to have along, but you don't stop being a Christian when you feel down.

We all *feel* rotten at times. But to *feel* rotten and to *act* rotten are two different problems. Don't merge them as one. [2]

---

[2] See Hebrews 11 for a cluster of examples of how this works.

3 *How can I be sure I'm placing my trust in a true thing? I'm getting my information secondhand, not from a voice out of a smoking mountain or a burning bush or something.*

Almost everything anyone believes is based on trusting an authority. For instance, you believe there is a place called Moscow, not necessarily because you've been there, but because reliable people have told you it's there. You have faith.

You get into your car and drive along a hilly road. Do you slow way down every time you approach the top of a hill because you're afraid there's no road on the other side? No, you trust your life to the road-builders. You believe in an authority. [1]

The best authority is Jesus Christ and His Word, the Bible. You can trust what He says.

When scientists built the cyclotron, they were working by faith to find incredibly small, short-lived energy particles which, by their calculations, should have existed. They had no proof. No one had seen one, nor a trail which one left behind. But mathematics indicated it should exist.

It did. The cyclotron proved the scientists' faith in a well-ordered universe.

The nature of things indicates God exists. His Word — which has the ring of truth — says Jesus Christ can be depended upon and followed with complete abandon.

---

[1] Read about Thomas' struggle with seeing vs. believing in John 20:19-31.

4 *I had God, but I can't find Him anymore. How come I feel so raunchy just when I need Him most?*

A lot of people ask this same question.

Have you really lost God? Or do you simply *feel* as if you have?

Of course, if you've neglected Him for a long period, you may be out of communication in a serious way. But if you communicate with Him again, He is going to respond.

Think of it this way. Some day you'll put your lips gently against the lips of the one you've just married.

Smile!
It won't last
forever

After the brief little kiss, some photos, cake ceremonies and rice-throwing, you'll drive off for your honeymoon. It will be like a sort of super-date. An unreal, beautiful experience, unique, emotional — you are finally together, finally able to fully express your love.

However, a few weeks later, after living together in the nitty-gritty of marriage, the relationship isn't quite on the same cloud. Still beautiful, hopefully, still a love relationship. But it's more *normal*. When you wake up in the morning, you won't always breathe deliciously and say, "Ah, you're here, let me hold your hand and dream, and let's talk about you and me." Instead, you'll probably stagger to the bathroom and wash your face as you do now.

Yet, you're still married. You still love. The fact you're together is still there, even if the emotions aren't quite the same ones which — as you drove away from the church — seemed to make all the world okay and *all* your problems solved. In actuality, your marriage may enable you to face your problems as a twosome and help you a great deal. At the same time, it gives you a whole new set of problems

However, the more you share with each other, the more you feel joy with each other. It's the same with God. Through prayer. Reading His Word. Sharing with your new brothers and sisters in Christ. God will do beautiful things in your life and at times give you a wonderful sense of His presence — but not always with honeymoon emotions.

If you still feel you can't find God, remember this. It is your *will* He is interested in. If you say with full conviction, "I *will* ask Christ to take over my life. I *will* obey what He tells me in the Bible. I *will* start specific actions right now to bring myself into line with what I know He wants. I *will* yield my body to Him." If you say all that, then no matter how lost you may *feel*, He'll be working in you, bringing you to full maturity. Emotions will tag along, depending on your personality, the situation and His working in you. [1]

[1] See John 2:18-22.

5 *Why is it so important to dedicate everything to Christ? Some people say you get neurotic worrying about every little detail. How much do I have to sacrifice for God? How hard do I have to try before it's enough?*

You are called to be a whole person. And you grow into that wholeness only through complete yielding to Christ.

You sacrifice everything — and you therefore gain everything. Halfway commitment fizzles. God intends to do the whole job in you.

It's like going out for football twenty pounds overweight. You might wish the coach would lay off. But

"Need
a
scale,
coach . . ."

he means to have you fit for play. You might want to complain, "Let me get by with a few things, Coach. Have a heart." But he's interested in accomplishing what you came to him for in the first place. And you have to do everything he says, or you're fooling yourself and failing him.

Again and again the Bible refers to Christ as "Lord." That means He's in charge. Of everything. Totally. Jesus commands us to obey Him and include Him. [1]

How do you get handles on that?

Agreed, it's a fuzzy sort of thing to talk about "yielding your life." What in the world does that mean? How do you go about it?

Concentrate on one thing at a time.

For instance, you may not know exactly what God wants to do in your future plans about college and marriage — but you do know how He wants you to act with your date this week. Jesus first came into your life by invitation. Now, invite Him into specific areas one at a time. If He's invited into your grades, then everything you do related to grades, He controls — and that's a victory point, a Jesus point, in your life. [2]

What's building the biggest barriers between you and God right now? Okay, concentrate on that one thing. Let's say it's your temper. Or your attitude toward your parents, or your brother, or your sister. Maybe it's your attitude toward school. Or the stuff you're reading in your spare time. Take one thing, bring it to the Lord and say, "Here it is. You come in, Lord. Take over. You're in charge."

If you've seen the film "The Longest Day" on TV, you know that in June of 1944, the Allies launched the biggest invasion in history — to take Europe. They didn't wildly try to capture everything at once. Eisenhower sent his soldiers in to set up beachheads.

A beachhead is one place you own. It's yours. A place from which to operate. A victory point. From one beachhead, you can go on and get one more small

[1] Luke 6:46-49.
[2] Philippians 2:12, 13.

victory, then another and another. That's what growth is all about.

Find something specific — something with a name, a time, a place. Say to God, "Here's the beachhead. I'm inviting You into that area to lead the battle." Jesus said in Matthew 6 that we're to live one day at a time. So today, take today's beach — and tomorrow another, always moving on as He leads you to full maturity and holiness.

As humans, we are never capable of 100 percent in anything. Give all of yourself to all you know of God. That's all you can do — and all God asks of you.

Give one area after another to Him. The basic law of growth is this: When you stop giving, you stop growing. When you keep on giving, you keep on growing.

There's always new ground to life. There's always something new to yield. And the more He controls, the more real He is to you, and the more rich and dynamic life becomes.

Jesus helps you accept yourself—
your fears and your failures.

6 *I've been trying awfully hard to be a Christian ever since I received Christ. But no matter how hard I try, I'm still not sure if God accepts me.*

A lot of kids get confused about the difference between trying to *become* a Christian and growth after being born into God's family. You don't have to work at becoming a Christian. If you've received Christ, you're one of His. God accepts you because of what Jesus did for you — not because you're a better kid. You can quit trying to *become* a Christian and get on with *growth*.

It's like the difference between discovering America — which was a one-time event — and exploring it. Columbus didn't have to go back and rediscover America every few months — that was accomplished fact. But exploration was a big, long, continuing job — a job which resulted in all sorts of major changes.

Goody
Twinkle
Shoes

7 *It seems things have just gotten worse for me since I've accepted Christ. I'm giving up stuff like making out and cheating. No X-rateds and all that. I'm practically Mr. Goody Twinkle Shoes. But it's tough, fighting against what you want to do all the time. I like what I've got in God, but life sure hasn't gotten any easier.*

Struggle is always a sign of life — and, usually, growth. The person who is content to sit still can usually slide along without the hassles . . . or the rewards.

It's like sports or exercise. You can sit around and do nothing, getting flabby. Or, you can move into the action. You grow stronger by stress, by pushing yourself till you hurt. You expect a little pain and unpleasantness when you're getting your body into shape.[1]

The Holy Spirit has breathed new life into your conscience. You're a brand-new person. Move into the challenge. Shove your face right up against some boulders that need to be moved! Place your feet on some tall mountains that need climbing!

[1] See the analogies of 2 Timothy 2:1-7.

Sure, a lot of kids prefer the easy way of stolen tests and easy makes at the drive-in. It's like some people who live to eat instead of eating to live. The food they gobble gives them a little pleasure, but it turns to a miserable weight around their middle. The person who learns to deny himself gets far more out of life and relationships — and even pleasures.

Of course, some people are quick to tell you that being a "holy Joe" is a drag. They tell you it's very dull next to some wild evenings. But true joy comes out of some pain, commitment and a direction in life. Ask any coach. Ask yourself in terms of what you really want in life.

Jesus gave you a mixed bag when you accepted Him. Denial of your selfishness. Commitment to living for others instead of self. His control of your body. All that may seem confining, but Jesus also said that the reason He came was to bring you joy. With Jesus, you have the fruits of the Spirit, which are "love, joy, peace, patience, kindness, goodness, faithfulness, gentleness and self-control." [2] Those are the kind of building blocks to build a life on, so you can move right into the rugged frustrations you'll face.

[2] Galatians 5:22, 23.

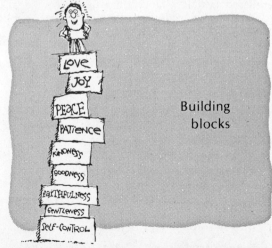

Building blocks

8 Does God change events and situations as well as attitudes? How does He work?

Most often you'll see God affecting events and situations *through* His changing of attitudes.

Recently, researchers have learned that if you change attitude, you change behavior. They had guessed that was so, but now their tests show it's for sure. For instance, if your attitude about a Gremlin or a Chevy — or a minority group or a cripple — can be changed, your behavior will change. You may buy a Gremlin (or be tempted to at least), and you may reach out to help a neighbor.

God moves in to change attitudes. Jesus said that the greatest commandment is, "Love the Lord your God with all your strength and all your might and all your mind, and your neighbor as yourself." That sort of attitude would change the world!

God also gets right into things directly. The "God who is there"[1] responds to specific requests and changes events and circumstances.

[1] See Francis Schaeffer's *The God Who Is There*. Inter Varsity Press).

Inherited grouchiness

9 *I have a terrible time getting good grades at school. Also, I blow up at my brother a lot. You see, I'm pretty insecure. I know I'm selfish and impatient. I want to care more about others and less about myself — but I'm not pulling it off. It's pretty discouraging when you're as irritable and dumb as I am.*

Let's assume you really are a grouch. Everybody considers you a pain, including you. But Joyce over there — she's naturally sweet and gracious.

Maybe she inherited that personality trait, the same as she inherited her dark hair and brown eyes and good hearing.

God intends to work with what you've got. He loves you as you are and has plans for you that go beyond what you can dream of.

Who is "better"? The kid who is very slow but gets C's or the bright guy who sloughs off and gets B's when he could get A's? Who is "better"? The asthmatic who kills himself to barely make second squad, or the jock who wants cheers for every little play?

29

10 *What does my new life have to do with the church? You say I'm into a "relationship and not merely religion." But where do the two meet? My church turns me off. And how can I justify the lack of unity in churches if Christ is its Leader?*

First, let's talk again about your being part of a new family. You have a large number of new brothers and sisters who love Christ. You've received quite a heritage. Ephesians 2:20-22 puts it this way: "What a foundation you stand on now: the apostles and the prophets, and the cornerstone of the building is Jesus Christ Himself! We who believe are carefully joined together with Christ as parts of a beautiful, constantly-growing temple for God. And you also are joined with Him and with each other by the Spirit, and are part of this dwelling place of God."

We need each other

30

A family is made up of very different sorts of people. Babies, grandfathers, teenagers, middle-agers. Each learns from the other. Each helps the other. A grandfather can do something for a teenager that his father can't. A baby can bring excitement into his mother's life as no one else can.

It's the same with the "body of Christ." His church is an *organism* — living, breathing people who are the "called-out ones," called out to Christ. You're incomplete without *all* the other members of this new family. You grow properly only as you interact in the family, as you love your brothers and sisters — especially the nagging, unlovable ones, for they're the ones who need love the most. (Remember — God loves you when you are unlovely.)

To grow, you need to see where you're going in life. What will it be like to be a parent? A home-builder? What's it like to face death at 70 when everybody is thinking, "I wish he'd die and get it over with — he's such a burden." Or to sit by your lover's bedside as cancer destroys your dreams? Or, to see the joy of a son getting married — or to watch your parents playing with your new-born baby brother. . . .

Growth requires breadth and depth. You are complete only with other Christians in whom God is working. [1]

If you see failure here, read what Galatians 6:1-3 advises: "Dear brothers, if a Christian is overcome by some sin, you who are godly should gently and humbly help him back onto the right path, remembering that next time it might be one of you who is in the wrong. Share each other's troubles and problems, and so obey our Lord's command. If anyone thinks he is too great to stoop to this, he is fooling himself. He is really a nobody."

[1] Read 1 Corinthians 12, Ephesians 4, Romans 12. Also, try *Body Life* by Ray Stedman (Gospel Light).

So, the church is not a group of plaster saints. They are people who need help and know it.

But what about the building on the corner — that place where you worship each week?

Let's look at it from two angles. First, your own responsibility.

Sun-kissed in the wheat field

Say you're out in a beautiful wheat field, running hand-in-hand with your beloved, and a photographer is clicking away with his camera. He's got this nutty idea that he can take fabulous photos of you and yours, looking blissful and sun-kissed, for a contemporary love poster. You've seen the wind-blown boy-girl posters in your drugstore, and you're putting on the same expressions as you dreamily run.

But let's say you're not really getting along that well with the beloved you're running hand-in-hand with so dreamily. Your relationship is full of put-downs. Well, you can run along for the camera. Everything looks great. But inside it's phony. Your true attitude toward the one you supposedly love is one of slicing and ungentle jabs.

It can be the same with your attitude toward a local church. (Let's hope it's not.) A lot of kids walk in, ready to judge and put down anything and everything, instead of reverently asking how God might speak to them. If your true relationship to Christ is cold and mechanical, then church will be, too. If your relationship to Christ is breathing and alive, then perhaps you'll find your church service also coming alive.

Set out to deliberately *create* fellowship. To show Christ's love.

Now, the other angle. It is true that many buildings on the corner and their congregations have lost something. Some have junked the very basics of believing in Christ and the Bible. Some don't know Christ at all. Others have turned mechanical. Still others have gone to another extreme — they push the right doctrine, but without love.

All of us find it easy to point out the problems. But what are some solutions?

Look at weakness as your opportunity. Pray for people within the church you attend. Pray for your minister.

Ask yourself, is it *all* their fault? Or is there something God wants to say to me through this?

You don't necessarily have to leave your church. You might find it more helpful to supplement it with other situations in which you can get together with brothers and sisters who are excited about God and can pass their excitement on to you.

Whatever you do, be sure to get with alive Christians regularly. It's a must — for spiritual growth and the inspiration to keep at it.

11 *I don't feel like I'm talking to the Lord the right way. And I know I'm doing some things that are wrong, but I keep doing them. In fact, I sin all over the place. I want to be constructively enthusiastic, but how can I control my attitudes and desires?*

Take some time to sit down and read what Jesus says in the Gospel of John, chapter 15. Read His explanations three times, slowly, and let the excitement of it soak into your inner self. You can't control your desires. But if you are like a branch on a tree, the life and God-control comes from the trunk. You find that you change, not so much from being ordered to, as from love and His life within you.

Unplugged

It's similar to a lamp. You have to plug it in. Unplugged, it may have a new filament and look very decorative. But it's dead. And a lamp can't plug itself in.

Ask Jesus to keep you plugged in continually. Then, the light will be coming from the Source. From Him. Your role is not to generate power or light, but to let it flow through you.

A student commented, "I find that when I'm plugged into God and talking to Him, my problems result in growth. But when I let the plug get gently pulled away or yanked out, my problems increase and get more frustrating. I get nowhere till I come back to talking to God."

12 *I keep feeling I'm going to fail — really bad, so that everybody will know it, and I'll look like an idiot. Will God let me fail?*

Maybe.

Before you knew Christ, the Bible says you were a slave to sin. You were God's enemy. Now, the Bible says, you're His child, you're specially beloved, you're free! [1]

And one of the things you're free to do is fail.

God is not nearly so interested in how you look in front of your friends (although He's not out to embarrass you) as He is in helping you grow into maturity. And sometimes failure is part of that. A father expects some knocks and bruises and stupidities on the part of his kids, but that's all normal development.

[1] Ephesians 2:1-10.

God has made you as you are—even if you don't have it all together. The great adventure is learning about the intricate you, with all your potential.

13 *Sometimes I'm the most confusing creature in the world. I do the dumbest things! I don't understand myself and why I do some of the things I do.*

Part of the great adventure with God is learning about the intricate, fascinating, marvelous you. God

Learning about you

is out to change us from larvae to butterflies — beautiful winged creatures to soar and flutter into the breeze. And He's starting with the unique raw *material* He created — you! In one sense, we're still in the caterpillar stage in that God has only begun His work in us humans. But learning what God has already made in you as a person is one of the great intrigues throughout your life. [1]

---

[1] For some really heavy reading on this, try *The Meaning of Persons* and *The Adventure of Living* by Paul Tournier (Harper and Row). Also see Romans 7:15-25.

Time
for
a
Reach Out

14 *How do I know that Christ really came into my life when I asked Him? I mean, my world didn't exactly change overnight or anything. How do I know I wasn't deluding myself and missed the real thing?*

Of course, it is possible you were only playing psychological games and not really yielding to Christ. But if you sincerely asked Him into your life and you're open to obeying Him, you can simply stand on the promise God gives: First John 5:9-13 says, "We believe men who witness in our courts, and so surely we can believe whatever God declares. . . . And what is it God has said? That He has given us eternal life, and that this life is in His Son. . . . I have written this to you who believe in the Son of God so that you may know you have eternal life."

Are things happening in your life that didn't happen before? Are you bothered by the way you treat your family sometimes? Do you feel like defending God or standing up for His Way more than you did? You will find clues in your own experience, changes in your life which you can't explain.

A student with a similar problem commented, "I talked with my club director's wife about it, and she said when she was super-messed up once, she prayed, 'God, if there is a God, prove to me that you are real, and help me.' He did it for her. So I did the same thing, and I was surprised when things worked out."

15 *I don't quite get this business of Christ doing everything and me just sitting around watching Him or something. Don't I have to do anything? And if I'm just supposed to open the door for Him, isn't that doing something?*

You are in a love relationship. It's not a fifty-fifty thing, but one in which Christ and you give all of yourselves to each other.

There's a creative tension between what God does for you and what you attempt yourself. [1] You'll find plenty of verses in your Bible or New Testament talking about what you should do. And plenty also about what God will do for you. Let God's Word, as you study it, give you a deeper and deeper understanding of the balance.

[1] Study 2 Peter 1:3-15.

16 *How do I start helping other kids experience all this? I really want to share it, 'cause they don't know what they don't have! But I'm afraid I won't have the words or the understanding to get it across.*

Begin by just naturally sharing what God has done for you.

Jesus once healed a blind man. The Pharisees — who didn't like Jesus — called the man in for interrogation, saying, "Give the glory to God, not to Jesus, for we know Jesus is an evil person." The once-blind man didn't have a lot of smart answers. He simply said, "I don't know whether He is good or bad, but I know this: *I was blind, and now I see!*" [1]

The man with new sight simply told what God had done for him, even when he was being cut down by

[1] John 9:25.

religious people who insisted they had all the answers. You don't have to know it all to share.

However, here are a few basics to get into your mind:

• Man's a bummer. No, he wasn't given a bum deal — *he's* the bummer because he's fighting God. Even now he spits in God's face with hatred, prejudice, injustice and war. And anybody who thinks *he's* not part of it should look inside himself.

• God wiped off the spit, and instead of smashing men, He sent His Son Jesus to bring truth and to die by man's evil hand. God is still wiping off the spit, yet He's still reaching out His loving hand to us.

• Jesus was sentenced to death because of our sins. He took the rap for us.

• To have peace with God, we have to invite Jesus Christ into our lives. We have to hate our evil actions and attitudes and let Him clean us up.

Emphasize to your friends how you don't feel you're better now. You're just one more rebel who has made his peace with God. You're just a "sinner saved by grace." As D. T. Niles of Ceylon puts it, "Evangelism is just one beggar telling another beggar where to find food." We're no better than terrorists or bigots or dope-pushers. We're all rebels.

Share what you understand, admitting you're just getting into this thing. And don't worry about the response — that's God's business. He will work in the lives of people in His timing as He wills. [2] Of course, your praying for your friends and showing them you care often triggers God's action. [3]

You're right that it's worth sharing. Even British writer and statesman John Morely, who didn't believe in Christ, saw what it would mean if Jesus was who He said He was. Morely stated, "If I believed that Jesus Christ was the Son of God and my Savior, I would never talk or write about anything else."

Your witnessing — that is, sharing what Christ has done for you and is doing — should be a by-product of living for Him. It just tags along naturally.

[2] 2 Corinthians 5:16-21 is possibly the best statement of your new role.

[3] Read *How to Give Away Your Faith,* by Paul Little (I-V Press).

17 *None of my friends accept what I say about Christ. They leave me out, and they brag about all the fun they have at their wild parties. They put me down because I don't drink or smoke. I feel hurt because I'm left out. I'm a drip at their parties. I want to be popular and feel secure — but how?*

Maybe it's time to find a whole new batch of friends. Check out Matthew 5:11, 12. Not everyone will love you or your faith.

18 *How can I change my reputation? I've been going to bed with guys, and the girls all hate me. They figure I'm still a tramp. I want to share my faith with these girls, but they'll hardly even talk to me.*

You probably won't be able to communicate much until they see a real difference in your life. You might as well accept that and allow God to time the sharing of your new life with them.

It's a bit like someone with bad cavities wanting to do a kiss-and-smile toothpaste commercial. After a trip to a dentist and an obvious change, maybe. . . .

If Christ is in control of your life, they'll see that bright new look and eventually start to show a different kind of interest. But it's also important that you get with other Christians so they can help you grow. Don't

The
bright
look

take too lightly the fact that your old friends can pull
you down. You are now a light in the world, Jesus
said. [1] But starting out, it's like carrying a little candle
through a dark night. If you are always sloshing
through a swamp, your candle is likely to get doused.
Get around people who also carry candles, and you'll
have light for your feet. You need people around who
are excited about Jesus and can share that excitement.

If you've been sleeping around a lot, you may want
to stop dating altogether for awhile. Temptations will
still be strong when you're out with a guy — particularly the wrong guy. Spend a few months concen-
trating on God's taking charge of every aspect of the
new you, and get involved in a whole new set of activities.

[1] Matthew 5:14-16.

Cold response

19 *I went out with this girl, and she heard I was a Christian, so now she's very cold to me. At work some of the guys think I'm on an ego trip because I'm always happy. My parents get mad at me and say I criticize them and I've changed for the worse. I feel I've changed for the better by following Christ.*

It's hard to be good. My parents keep putting me down — they think I'm going through a phase. Actually, I feel I'm a pretty bad Christian. I'm afraid to talk about it because then, when I don't want to clean the garage or something, they throw it back at me: "Fine Christian you are!"

You've hit some tough reactions. Of course, a current slogan isn't too bad a response to your parents' jibe: "Please be patient. God isn't finished with me yet." As a newborn Christian, you're not saying you're the golden good boy, but someone who wants to improve and has opened himself to God for help.

Love your parents as they are. That's part of your

challenge. Love them with the idea that God — not you — will change them. Accept the fact they won't understand and that a lot of the rest of the world won't either. But as you live it out day by day and month by month, people will see a difference. By admitting you're not so good, you're showing the right attitude for growth.

A boy who was finding that he just couldn't communicate with his family adapted St. Francis' prayer this way: "Lord, grant me the grace and love to be still (but pray) before my parents when I'm right . . . and grant me the humility to admit to them my sins when I'm wrong."

Living with people is the challenge God has given us. It's a bigger challenge than the decathlon or the Super Bowl. And only God can help you head into it and win some victories.

The put-down. How do you react to people who reject — even make fun of — your faith?

Still there, God?

20 *Frankly, I don't know how to pray. I say, "Hello, God." Then there's this long silence. What should I say?*

There's no mysterious formula. In fact, you might start at the most natural point — what you're already thinking about. Is it a test tomorrow? A teacher who put you down? Your best friend who's having troubles and taking them out on you? A trip you're going on? A date you're excited about?

God wants to be in on all aspects of your life — the laughter and the good times, as well as the fears and frustrations. Bring up whatever's most important to you right then. Like, "Lord, I think I'm getting too involved with Lindy. It scares me. What should I do?" Or, "Father, you know I just can't stand Dwight. Sometimes I scream inside! How do I handle myself?"

Invite God into the real stuff of your life! You'll find He'll answer your prayers in many ways. Through circumstances. Through other Christians. Through His Word.

Let the Bible blend into your prayers. For instance, say you're really afraid to get up in class to give a speech. You'll find the promise "God hath not given us the spirit of fear; but of power, and of love, and

46

of a sound mind" relates to you right then. One student we know always repeats that promise [1] when he has to talk in front of a group, praying to God to make it happen. "The promise comes true," he says. "I'm much more self-confident as I include God when I'm scared. It gets my mind off me and my making a good impression. He keeps me from being so self-centered, and He really does help me to think clearly."

God cares about the things you care about. Talk to Him about anything and everything. He's the God who created Earth, Mars and the Milky Way, but He also made tiny microbes. Jesus said He even cares about the hairs on your head. God lived here Himself, and He knows what it's like. Jesus invaded Planet Earth not to swagger around and play Superstar, but to feel toothaches and hear people cut Him down. He shared the temptations, despair and pleasures you now have. He knows what you're going through, and He'll move in beside you. Even when you don't feel like talking to Him, tell Him about that, too. He already knows you, thought for thought.

That's
a
door?

You'll find that as you bring Him your biggest problems, they'll become — believe it or not — the best things in your life. They're doors you shove open in desperation for Him to enter your innermost self and work miracles at the core of the real you. [2]

Pray for others, too, of course. To truly love someone, you want God's best for him. A way to see that happen is to ask God to work in his life.

You'll also want to praise God. And thank Him for the things He's already done in your life. Gratitude — according to a hospital study — is the healthiest emotion known to man. You'll find it's at moments when you show your gratitude to God that you'll find your greatest joys.

A student commented, "Whenever I face difficult problems or large decisions, I ask God to help me. I'm so glad to have Christ there! He's like an older Brother, or a Person you can tell your secrets to and not worry about their getting blabbered about."

[2] Philippians 4:4-7 is a wide-open invitation to do just this.

21 *Sometimes I feel weird, sitting in my room talking to a wall or a window. Or shutting my eyes and talking to the dark. Is God really there? At times I feel like I'm having a conversation with empty space.*

Yes, God is there, whether you feel Him or not.

Actually, your feelings probably have more to do with things like a rotten day at school, or an A on a paper, or a fight with a friend, or a new outfit you just bought than with God's location. One day, perhaps, you found something exciting in the Bible. Another day you haven't thought about God once. All sorts of events affect your feelings.

You know He's there—live, powerful. But how do you make contact?

God is most interested in your *will* — not your emotions. You should feel free to say, "Lord, to be truthful, I don't even feel like talking to You. I don't feel like You're in the room. I don't feel like You've been doing anything in my life today. But I need You, that's sure. If You want to change me, here I am. Work on me any way You want. In fact, I pray that You will!"

Actually, God is most delighted with His sons and daughters — and you are one! — as they seek Him when they feel out of it. It's easy to pray when you're spiritually high. But all Christians go through dry periods. Thomas à Kempis, author of *The Imitation of Christ*, said he didn't know a Christian who didn't have them. Bible translator J. B. Phillips had a severe case of the spiritual blahs which lasted for years, but finally lifted. You'll have times when you don't know if God is around or not, too. That's just the time to defeat Satan by saying, "God, I don't know what's coming off, but here I am. I believe in You. Keep working in my life."

And He will — in His own way, in His own time.

22 *I want to spend time talking to God every day. But I put it off. Before I know it, I'm sacked out, and I haven't had my quiet time. And when I do pray, my mind wanders. I've even fallen asleep!*

Walking and talking

Try walking while you pray. One guy we know always does his talking with God while taking a 20-minute walk each evening. And, if your mind wanders — let it! Simply invite Jesus to go along for the ride. Let's face it, God knows what your mind is doing all the time. During your quiet time, He's not surprised to see your mind wandering. Ask Him to take charge of your time with Him and control your thoughts. You might keep a note card and pencil with you to jot things down when you pray, like, "Oh, I have to remember to talk to Bob tomorrow!" Write it down; then you can forget it and get back to the business at hand.

The whole question of having a set time to meet God is a little tougher. Many Christians would tell you that after years of struggle, they haven't found a magic answer. But here are some thoughts which should be helpful:

• *God wants to relate to you all day.* Make little sentence prayers and thoughts run through your activities. Like, "Uh oh, here comes George, and I don't know what to say to him! Help me, Lord!" Or, "Wow! You know, God, I'm really enjoying this ball game. Thank you, Jesus, for my health and for all you're doing in me, even if I am still full of faults."

In other words, don't limit your prayers to a formal quiet time.

• *On the other hand, setting aside time each day can change your life.* Remember Daniel in the Old Testament — the one thrown into a den of lions who came out alive? He ran kingdoms and was quite a hero for God. And he prayed three times a day. [1] (In fact, that's what got him thrown to the lions.) It was a habit which kept him so close to God that the Lord called Daniel especially beloved.

Most Christ-followers find it helpful to set a time and place to be alone with God. It might be walking a mile or so, or kneeling in your room, or sitting in a quiet corner of the library, or staying in your car. Bring your Bible with you. Mix talking with God with His talking to you through His Word. And when you miss a day or two, don't get upset. Just start again and ask for God's help. Ask Him, "How do You see this building a habit of time with You? How can You help me, Lord?" You're not chained to endless self-effort. Nor should you feel bound to a legalistic system. Ask God what will work for you. The important thing is to be in regular communication with Him.

• *Remember, you are meeting a Person, Someone who really cares about you and wants to talk with you.*

[1] Daniel 6.

Batless Babe

Jesus loves you and wants to share His exciting plans for your growth. When you spend time with Him, you're always richer for it.

In a way, the Christian who does not talk to God is like Babe Ruth without a bat. What a waste! Your communication with God gives you the zip and snap and purity and insights to really live in the middle of a mixed-up world. As one student said, "Last night, I had doubts about my needing Christ. He'd been sort of a 'good-luck charm' to get into heaven with. But all of a sudden, after I'd prayed seriously, I burst out crying, realizing that I needed Him every day!"

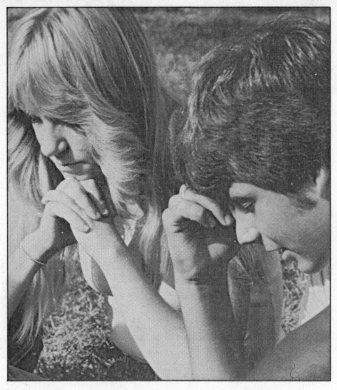

Prayer lets God get involved right
where you and your friends live.

23 *Just how much power is there in prayer? Could I pray for someone to be healed of cancer and see it happen? Somehow, that seems way out of reach. In fact, getting specific answers at all seems beyond me.*

There is power in prayer. Jesus said: "If you live in Me — abide vitally united to Me — and My words remain in you and continue to live in your hearts, ask whatever you will and it shall be done for you." [1]

Jesus' followers experienced the following:

"And when they had prayed, the place in which they were assembled was shaken." [2]

God says through Jeremiah:

"Call unto me, and I will answer thee, and shew thee great and mighty things, which thou knowest not." [3]

God is prepared to answer your requests. But it's not a magic show, and it's not a matter of manipulating Him to do things. You may ask that someone be cured of cancer, for instance, but you fit into His will, not He into yours. He may answer your prayer miraculously, or He may make you wait to see His different plan.

God is at work in you to shape you and bring you to full maturity. Prayer is the nerve center for the process. It's far more than your drawing up a list of requests and His answering them. Prayer is getting to

---

[1] John 15:7, *Amplified Bible.*
[2] Acts 4:31, *Amplified Bible.*
[3] Jeremiah 33:3, KJV.

know His will for you — what He really wants — and then accepting that. You'll find that's the most exciting plan in the long run.

You don't feel you believe God enough for "big things"? You don't believe, for instance, that if you asked God to bring your friend to Himself that He

"One more thing God . . ."

REQUESTS

would do it? Then perhaps you should start with what you do believe He'd do. If you asked Him to help you say one thing to your friend about Christ this week, do you believe He could do that? After He's done that, could you believe God would answer your prayers and help you give him a New Testament or some Christian literature in a way that seemed very natural? Do you think, eventually, you could believe God for opening up just the right situation for you to share with him what Christ means in your life now?

Or, say you have a problem with your temper. You know God isn't going to totally defuse you. But could you believe He will keep you from making sharp remarks — just help you to keep your mouth shut — next time you get ticked off?

The idea is to take *faith-sized requests* — what you believe God can and will do if you ask — and then watch Him work. You have some faith. It's enough. (Ask for more, and God will give it.)

Make your requests very specific. You might want to keep a little notebook — write down your requests on one column, and as they are answered, check them off, with the date it happened and perhaps a comment. [4]

Consider the first two verses of Psalm 116:

"I love the Lord because He hears my prayers and answers them. Because He bends down and listens, I will pray as long as I breathe!"

Archbishop Temple, when told all of his answers to prayer were probably coincidences, made an interesting comment: "Maybe so. But when I quit praying, the coincidences stop happening."

[4] To inspire your faith, take a half hour some time and look up these verses in the New Testament. Read each one slowly, several times. See what God will say to you through them: Matthew 6:8; 7:7-12; 18:18-20; 21:21, 22; Mark 11:22-26; Luke 11:9-11; John 14:12-14; 15:7; 16:24; James 1:5-8; 1 John 3:20-22; 5:14, 15.

Not
toy
robots

24 *I have a question that's really bothering me, even though it may seem silly to you. It's this: Why pray at all? If God knows what we need, why ask Him for it? Can't He just give it to us without our having to run to Him about every little thing?*

But that's the whole idea — running to Him with every little thing. If the God of the universe is interested enough to care, who are we to ignore Him? "Every little thing" is just what God wants to be part of, for your every breath is sustained by Him.

As you let God in, you're saying about your desire to run your own show, "Lord, I know I'm self-centered. Take your knife. Cut! Slice out the malignancy I know is in me. Graft in your green shoots of life. Let your love sprout in everything I do!"

To go any other route as a Christian is to say, "Why do *anything*? Why hospitals? Why give bread to the hungry? Why exert myself at all? God knows it's needed." But the Lord doesn't work that way. He chose to make us significant — not toy robots. We are His muscles, His eyes, His voice. He works through us and through our prayers. Certainly He isn't limited to working that way. But He chooses us as participants — and that's exciting! God works through us in various ways, and our prayer releases His power. [1]

James said, "You have not because you ask not." [2]

---

[1] Jesus talked about this very question in His *Sermon on the Mount;* see Matthew 6:5-15.

[2] James 4:2.

25 *Frankly, God hasn't exactly come through for me on everything. I've asked Him for some pretty special things that were very important to me, and God sort of dropped the ball. I don't mean to be irreverent or anything, but how come He doesn't always come through?*

Watch out you don't make the mistake of considering God your Heavenly Errand Boy.

Actually, getting involved with God means radical surgery in your life. A large part of prayer is tuning yourself to His will so you'll be asking for what He wants. Psalm 37:4 says, "Delight thyself also in the Lord; and he shall give thee the desires of thine heart." Notice the beautiful cycle here. You delight yourself in God. You're excited about Him. Okay, that means you're naturally delighted with things He's happy with. In a relationship like that, the Psalmist says God will give you your desires.

You are a rebel who has laid down his rifle and bayonet. God is now your Leader — that's why you call Him Lord. You may, perhaps, resent that, but accepting His authority over you is the way to genuine freedom. To seeing God work miracles in your life. After all, He made you. He breathes life into you.

Here are some reasons for unanswered prayers:

• *Obstructions between you and God.* Sin blocks your communication. For instance, if you're unwilling to forgive someone who's hurt you, why should God forgive you? Why should He do what you ask when Jesus said you should forgive others? If you can't forgive someone, ask God to move in and change you. Only He can. Confess your sins, ask for His cleanup.

Then, stop condemning yourself. If Christ has forgiven you (and He promises to every time you ask), [1] then surely you can. Jesus said He came that you might have joy. Forgive yourself when He forgives!

Giving her what she wants

• *God's view is different from yours.* Have you ever had to take care of a baby sister, or babysit as a job? You watch the kid trying to get into everything. She tries to stick her wet fingers into the electric outlet. "No!!!" you scream. She looks up at you like you're a drag. *Spoilsport!* Then she starts wailing. Later, the kid may want all sorts of things, but you'll give her only what you know is best for her. You give her one of three answers to each request: Yes, No or Wait. And, if at all possible, you'll say "yes."

Our Father wants to give us "the desires of our heart." But He knows what is best for us — to mature, to fit into His mosaic. Only He knows when a prayer is like putting wet fingers into electricity. Only He knows the right time to say "No." Or "Wait." Or "Yes." [2]

[1] 1 John 1:9.
[2] See Isaiah 55:6-13.

We can talk to God better when we understand that His view of us is completely different from our own.

Of course, as you keep praying, you may find you'll change your requests. Or things may change, and you'll wonder what made you ask for that in the first place! The point is, keep on asking. Prayer is changing you as well as the people around you.

Jesus asked once, "Why do you call me Lord, yet don't do the things I say?" Are you obeying Christ so He can work through you? Or, perhaps you have doubts that He'll do anything at all. If so, tell Him exactly that, then ask for more faith.

Remember this: Jesus Himself, in Gethsemane, prayed three times that a bitter cup of troubles would pass from Him. But the Father told Him to drink it, and Jesus obeyed Him. The Father answered Jesus' prayer, but not according to His original request.

26 *I'm getting a lot out of talking to God by my-self. But I'm afraid to do it with somebody else — in a group, I mean. Is it really necessary to pray with other Christians?*

You'll be missing out if you don't.

It's interesting that the Lord's Prayer which Jesus gave His followers says, "give us our daily bread. . . . forgive us. . . ." Jesus said, "Where two or three are gathered together in my name, there am I in the midst of them." [1]

You need your personal prayers alone. But sharing with others enriches you in a unique way. Enjoying God, agreeing to do what He wants, asking Him to change things — these are community experiences. You may not be able to see God, but you can see your Christian brother. Here is flesh-and-blood contact to encourage you.

If you feel a bit awkward praying aloud in a group, pray silently. And, perhaps you'll want to meet regularly with just one friend who will be your prayer-partner. He can help you keep up the discipline of prayer — you can share your deepest concerns with each other.

Know anybody who needs your prayer interaction as much as you need his?

[1] Matthew 18:20.

"I don't give a rip"

27 *To be honest, I don't pray very much. For instance, I know I should pray that Bob will accept Christ, but when I'm honest, I might as well admit I don't give a rip about Bob. The things I'm supposed to be praying about bore me. So I don't pray.*

You've taken the first step — being honest. Now, tell the same thing to God. He knows what you're interested in and what you're bored by. Forget about the things you're "supposed" to be praying about, and talk to Him about your sex life or your last talk with your parents or your grades. You'll find that as you include Him in your interests, in the real you, He'll begin to develop your concern for others.

Actually, you can't make yourself care about Bob. Only God can do that. And He'll get around to that if you talk to Him about your deepest concerns and ask Him to fill you with His Spirit.

Maybe the real reason you don't pray is that you're afraid He'll start meddling. Perhaps you don't want Him "nosing around" in certain areas He'll want to change. We all feel that way at times, you know. But it's no good to pretend you can hide anything. He knows all about your failures. And if you don't invite Him into every corner of your life, you'll miss out on the growing, joyful life He's promised you.

Open up, and let God. . . .

28 *Someone told me I should pray for people I can't stand. I guess it sounds like a good idea, but to tell you the truth, I don't really want to.*

Of course you don't — none of us do. We'd rather dislike a person, and we know that if we start praying for him, that has to change. Yet Jesus commanded us to love our enemies. [1]

Rosalind Rinker comments, "I will love God only as much as I love the person I dislike the most." You may think that's too strong. But we are all in the same boat — we're all sinners. Any nastiness you see in someone else is no worse than the badness you're capable of. We are fallen creatures.

At the same time, we are made in God's image. C. S. Lewis tells us, "I once talked to a pastor who had seen Hitler, and had, by all human standards, good cause to hate him. 'What did he look like?' I asked. 'Like all men,' he replied. 'That is, like Christ.' "

Most of us think of Hitler as an arch-fiend, and perhaps he was. But do we think of him as worse than ourselves? Do we think of him as someone whom Christ could *not* have transformed? When we consider ourselves far more deserving of joys in Christ than "bad people," we are on dangerous ground. British preacher John Bradford saw a drunken bum on the street and commented, "There, but for the grace of God, go I."

We are often hurt by people. We are infuriated. We sulk. We plot revenge. We gossip about "dumb

[1] Try on Matthew 5:43-48!

toads." But this is precisely where God wants to invade us, to change us. Praying for our "enemies" enables Him to transform us dramatically.

Jacob DeShazer, in a Japanese prison in World War II, got a Bible and accepted Christ through reading it. Later, he read Jesus' command, "Love your enemies." DeShazer's enemy was the cruel guard who had just slammed a heavy, iron-barred door on his bare ankle. But, Jesus said to love him — regardless of the pain. The next morning, DeShazer talked pleasantly to the guard, asking about his family. Through small, loving acts, the prisoner built up a friendship which became a beautiful work of God instead of a festering resentment.

Why not try it? List three people you dislike the most. Or can't get along with. Maybe it's even someone in your family. Put their names with other prayer requests in your Bible. Pray for them — for God to work in their lives. Then see what God will do to your own attitudes.

Heavy, man

29 *Okay, so I have this big Book in my hand. You say it's only part of the Bible — the New Testament. But it still looks thicker than any other book I've read in my life! Where in the world do I start? Just dig right in, like a novel or something?*

You could read it straight through, but here's another suggestion. Start with the letter called First John. It was written by Jesus' best friend, and the theme is love — both toward God and those around us. You'll find it pretty down-to-earth.

Over a period of days, read it through several times. Then, turn back a little further to the letter written by James, who was Jesus' brother. It, too, is down-to-earth and gets you thinking about how all this gets into your life.

Next, read Mark. This is a young man's account of Jesus' life — what He did and said. Take your time — don't feel you have to "plow through." After Mark, read these letters: 1. Ephesians. 2. Romans. 3. Colossians. 4. Philippians.

30 *I'm not quite sure I understand what the Bible is supposed to do for me. Why should I read it so much?*

You'll soon find that the Bible is a major way of God's speaking to you. It's His Book.

Your new love relationship with God makes you want to know what He has to say. If you were going with someone who, say, had moved to France — and you were really in love — you can be sure that the arrival of a letter from Paris would be a very special moment. You'd wish a letter would arrive every day, and you'd eagerly open it and read it. Then you'd read it a couple more times to be sure you knew exactly what it said and what was behind the comments.

It's the same with God's letters to you. No, it's not in personal letter form. But when you keep asking, "How does this apply to *me?*" you'll find it coming alive. It becomes spiritual food! [1]

In a way, you're like a sports car made to run on high-octane fuel. Yes, you can pour cheap junk into the tank. You can even put in crankcase oil, and perhaps it will cough along. *Maybe.* But for it to run with full power — to roar around the oval as it was meant to — it needs the explosive stuff.

You were made for the fuel God provides in His Word. It's not the only way He empowers you and speaks to you, but it's the gas pump nearest you, and always available. Ignore it, and you will cough along

[1] See 2 Timothy 3:14-17; also Jesus' story about the farmer in Matthew 13:19, 18-23.

through life or perhaps conk out as a Christian. (You probably know people hung up on the shoulder of the road.)

Running on full power

Spiritual food is not just a nice idea — it's a necessity. We've all seen photos of people dying of starvation. Pitiful! Emaciated. And that's what a Christian is like without spiritual food — especially when he's beginning his Christian life and doesn't have a lot of reserves to fall back on.

How often do you need this spiritual food? Well, there's no cut-and-dried answer, but compare it to actual proteins and carbohydrates and vitamins. At the last camp or weekend retreat you attended, how regularly did you and the other kids eat? At a camp last summer, a glorious array of roast beef, mashed potatoes, corn, salad, rolls, soft drinks and cherry pie were laid out for supper. The kids put enough away for sixty elephants. "Man, I won't be able to eat for a week!" was said in different ways at every table. The next morning, however, breakfast was a half-hour late. The campers were starving as they stood in line — some practically fell to the floor, gripping their stomachs in withdrawal pains.

Food's a constant necessity. It's the same with your spiritual needs, except for one thing. You aren't compelled by hunger pangs to get what you need. It's more like fuel for your gas tank — you don't always put it in 'cause it's so much fun hearing it gurgle down the pipe. You put it in when the gauge says empty because you know the consequences of no power. It's not always convenient to stop at a gas station — but you do anyway, even if it makes you a bit late to wherever you're going.

Which is why you should try to set up your Bible reading and talking to God at a certain time each day — so that it will become a habit, like brushing your teeth or washing your face. Once you build a habit, it takes over for you and becomes part of routine. The toughest part is getting the habit set up and a regular part of you.

This habit — once in your life — will change it. Not that you'll never miss a day or so, nor that it should become a ritual. You're not out to prove anything. It's simply scheduling a spiritual breakfast or dinner. Also, take advantage of any time you're not extra busy. Maybe Saturday or Sunday. Make your schedule practical, and keep working at it, because in our ultra-busy society, it's not easy.

Enough
for
sixty
elephants

How do you know when you're spiritually under-nourished? You'll feel more and more like saying, "Ahh, I don't care." That's the danger sign. After that comes disgust with yourself and your running your own life, and that may or may not bring you back into enriching fellowship with Him.

Why read the Bible so much? It's your true guide to action and attitudes. His Holy Spirit will speak to you through it and give you hope.

Billy Graham tells the story of the time he was invited to No. 10 Downing Street in London by Sir Winston Churchill. It was during a time of deep discouragement for the Prime Minister. After greeting Graham, the Briton asked, "Young man, do you have any hope for the world?" The evangelist took a New Testament from his pocket and said, "Mr. Prime Minister, this book is full of hope." He asked Graham to read some passages, and for the next 30 minutes he did. As Graham left, the Prime Minister said to him warmly, "I thank you. You have given an old man a renewed faith for the future." Graham later commented, "I hadn't. But the Bible had."

Look around. You see despair. Frustration. Bitterness. Bleak expressions on cynical faces. We are all infected with the drag of living in a broken, fallen world. But the Bible offers hope. Not some mealy-mouthed, Pollyanna, everything-is-roses farce. It offers hope in the middle of deceit and rage and revenge and shattered love between man and woman. You will, in fact, find an almost chilling realism in the Bible. It paints the human scene precisely as we find it today. Yet you will not find one of its sixty-six books without hope. God keeps saying in the Bible, "Look to Me. You will find rest and peace. Truth to hold on to. Repent of your sins. Take up your cross and follow Me."

31 *I watch other people who seem to be forever quoting verses from the Bible that "leaped out at them" or something. I don't think I'll ever be able to relate to the Bible like that. I'm afraid I'm a dud — I just don't get that much out of it.*

Do you have a modern edition? The *Reach Out New Testament* and *The Way* — the Living Bible — are paraphrases which are especially helpful to a new Christian. [1] The original Greek of the New Testament was street language — not at all refined — so common, everyday language you can understand is a logical first step.

Of course, some people do have a special knack for seeing things in Scripture which they can apply to themselves. And they want to share these insights. It would be dishonest to say you will be able to see things just as clearly as anyone else. Each of us has specific talents.

But you can train your mind and stretch it! Here are some tips:

Your frame of mind is vital. Remember, this is God speaking to you. Ask Him to show you what it means for your life. Then, be ready to obey. If you're open to His leadership, He's obviously more apt to give it.

[1] Translations you might want to get: *Good News for Modern Man* (Today's English Version) is available in inexpensive paperback; *The Berkeley Translation* (Zondervan); *The New Testament in Modern Language* by J. B. Phillips (Macmillan).

73

But in a world of class schedules, tests, ball games, and dates how can the Bible relate? Can it make your hectic world better?

Make prayer and Bible reading become a living inter-action. You may be in the middle of a Psalm and feel you want to talk to God about what it's saying. Good! That's what it's all about.

God speaks when you're awake

Don't just chew — *swallow!* It would be rather silly for you to sit at dinner and carefully chew your meat forty times per bite but never swallow it. Yet that's how a lot of people relate to the Bible. Knowing the facts and what they say is helpful—but you have to apply them to your life.

How do you do that? Well, you want God to affect your relationship with, say, your mother. But she — obviously — isn't mentioned in Scripture.

So — what do you do?

As an example, take the following statements from the first chapter of James. Read them slowly, thoughtfully:

"Dear brothers, is your life full of difficulties and temptations? Then be happy, for when the way is rough, your patience has a chance to grow. So let it grow, and don't try to squirm out of your problems. For when your patience is finally in full bloom, then you will be ready for anything, strong in character, full and complete." [2]

[2] James 1:2-4.

75

Okay. How do you swallow that?

Let's go back to your mother, whom we'll assume for the illustration that you've been having some sharp disagreements with. Okay, put her name in there.

"Is your life full of Mother?"

"Is your life full of mother? Then be happy, for when the way is rough, your patience has a chance to grow. And don't try to squirm out of your problems with mother. For when your patience toward her is finally in full bloom, then you will be ready for anything, strong in character, full and complete."

If the Bible is talking about sin, ask yourself, "Which sin?" If it's talking about loving a brother, ask yourself, "Which brother?" Put your own name in often. Constantly apply to yourself everything you read — whether it's advice or a story about someone. What hatreds or lusts or stupidities is this person guilty of that I can avoid? What love did this other person show that I could copy?

32 *This may sound like a stupid little question, but you keep referring to things like (John 1:12) and (Ephesians 2:8,9). I don't get it. Are they like chapters in a regular book? Or do they divide up like Shakespeare or something?*

If you're not familiar with the different books of the Bible, look at the very beginning, and you'll notice them all listed there for you. About 700 years ago or so, each "book" was put into chapters and small chunks called verses for easy reference. Each book is either a letter or piece of history or a series of songs (the Psalms) or biography, like the Gospel of John. The colon (:) is the divider that splits chapter numbers from verse numbers. Try looking up a few of these references like John 3:16 with the aid of your front index. You'll find it relatively easy.

33 *Do I have to accept everything in the Bible and all Christian doctrine to be a true Christian? I've received Christ, but there are a lot of things I have doubts about.*

You will for the rest of your life! Satan will whisper them to you, but it will also be the natural result of looking at all sides of the arguments.

If you were to pretend you don't doubt anything, you'd be naive. Your doubts are not sin if they are honest questionings.

In fact, treat them as opportunities. Bring them right into the open, and ask Christian leaders the hard questions. Especially confront God with them. He knows what the tough conundrums of the universe are and the paradoxes of Scripture. [1]

Then, relax. Follow Him and ask Him to lead your mind. He will! The Psalmists and Job and other men in Scripture question God and are eventually brought to truth. That's the real stuff of life, and God expects you to participate as doubts arise.

And remember this — you can't expect to know it all. Only God Himself does. As G. Wallace Hamilton has said, "He who wants all heaven in his head is going to get his head split."

[1] Read *Basic Christianity* by John Stott (Inter-Varsity Press), *Mere Christianity* by C. S. Lewis (Macmillan), *Know What You Believe* and *Know Why You Believe* by Paul Little (Victor Books).

A split head

34 *The thing I can't understand about the Bible is all the violence in the Old Testament. Such as God sending the Israelites into cities to kill men, women and children — stuff like that. How could a God of love command such things? Also, haven't a lot of people used the Bible to "prove" stupid things, like black people being not as good as whites?*

The Old Testament must be viewed — like all Scripture — from God's point of view. Man rebelled. "Men, women and children," whole cities and cultures — in fact, all of Adam's descendants — lived as depraved rebels whose life-styles "stunk in God's nostrils." [1]

God chose a group of these rebels to work in. They were Israelites — the Jews — and God's plan was to bring about a whole new life-style. He moved into their brutalizing ways and gave a set of laws that would provide for widows and orphans, and free slaves, and protect neighbors and strangers. And most of all, His Way commanded them to "love the Lord their God with all their hearts, souls, minds and strength."

When these chosen Israelites lived side-by-side with people who were still enemies of God, He knew they would contaminate His chosen people into becoming traitors. The rebels weren't about to move on, so God gave the command to destroy them. [2]

[1] Isaiah 65:1-12 is one example.
[2] Deuteronomy 9:4, 5.

79

All of this points up the deadly seriousness of life and death, our rebelliousness and God's claims upon us. The scenes are not easily glossed over, and the questions they raise are not simplistically answered. We're not in a little playground here on earth — we are significant humans with important choices to make — and the consequences are enormous.

Author David Winter [3] comments that the main criticism we have of this bloodshed is based on the belief that death is the worst thing that can happen to a person. But perhaps allowing evil to continue is even worse. Certainly to be an enemy of God is worse than death. We see in the Old Testament not only God's love and concern, but His judgment, His blazing holiness, the terrible reality of our fall from God.

And this doesn't contradict Jesus. True, He loves us. He died for us. But Jesus spoke about hell as well as heaven.

It's dangerous to bring our ideas to the Bible and try to mold it — instead of letting it mold us. True, men have used the Bible to "prove" blacks are inferior.[4] It's also true you can "prove" almost anything from the Bible. Take verses from here and there, patch them together, and a man can lay a case for almost any wild theory. In fact, that's why so many cults can say they are based on the Bible; they actually misuse it, instead of letting the Bible form them.

A humorous example often given is this one: A man looked up a verse: "Judas went and hanged himself." Then he flipped to another verse: "Go thou and do likewise."

Obviously, the rest of the Bible must be considered when you look at one part of it.

[3] Author of *Now What?*, a very helpful book for the new Christian, available in paperback from Harold Shaw Publishers, Wheaton, Ill.

[4] See Colossians 3:11 for Paul's view.

Let it mold your thinking — *not* vice versa. Compare all of Scripture and see how it blends together.

The Bible is an incredibly realistic assortment of different types of literature, all with a common theme. You will meet mysteries and mindbenders — things that will keep you going deeper and deeper till you're old and gray. That's one way you can tell it's God's Word. No shallow answers can sum it up. There are enigmas to be probed and tough things to swallow.

In this, as in all questions, confront God. Ask Him to show you directly from His Word just why He acts the way He does. And just what He means by each statement.

35 *You tell me that the Bible is God's Word. That's quite a claim! Is that a bit much? I want to believe it, but I've heard about scientific contradictions and differing views.*

Probably the most famous single C. S. Lewis quote is this from *Mere Christianity:* "A man who was merely a man and said the sort of things Jesus said would not be a great moral teacher. He would either be a lunatic — on a level with the man who says he is a poached egg — or else he would be the Devil of Hell.

A poached egg?

You must make your choice. Either this Man was, and is, the Son of God; or else a madman or something worse. You can shut Him up for a fool; you can spit at Him and kill Him as a demon; or you can fall at His feet and call Him Lord and God. But let us not come with any patronizing nonsense about His being a great human teacher. He has not left that open to us. He did not intend to."

That's quite a thought! And you must make almost the same statements about the Bible. To say it's merely great literature or that it contains some beautiful ideas to enrich life will not do. The Bible claims to be far more than that. Either the people writing it were the greatest egomaniacs to ever sit down with quill and scroll, or they were hopelessly deluded — or they actually were writing down words that were "God-breathed." Consider what the writers themselves say:

"The whole Bible was given to us by inspiration from God and is useful to teach us what is true and to make us realize what is wrong in our lives; it straightens us out and helps us do what is right." [1]

"For no prophecy recorded in Scripture was ever thought up by the prophet himself. It was the Holy Spirit within these godly men who gave them true messages from God." [2]

Again and again the Bible [3] claims to be speaking God's words. And Jesus Himself referred to Scriptures as authoritative, even supporting the story of Jonah and the great fish. [4]

You'll find many other reasons for believing the Bible to be accurate, genuine and truly inspired by God. [5] But to sum up, here are several paragraphs from a *Reader's Digest* article by Billy Graham:

"As astronauts Borman, Lovell and Anders were circling the moon and sending back descriptions of celestial glories seen from 230,000 miles in space, they suddenly introduced in their report a feature not programmed in either Houston or Cape Kennedy. They

[1] 2 Timothy 3:16.
[2] 2 Peter 1:20 and 21.
[3] See Jeremiah 1:9; 1 Corinthians 14:37; 1 Thessalonians 2: 13; 2 Samuel 23:1-3; Ezekiel 3:4; Micah 3:8; 2 Peter 3:2.
[4] See Matthew 12:40; 5:18 and John 10:35.
[5] For facts about the Bible, see F. F. Bruce's *New Testament Documents: Are They Reliable?*, available in paperback from Wm. B. Eerdmans Publishers, Grand Rapids, Mich.

Unexpected
Apollo
report

began reading, reverently, the Biblical account of the Creation: 'In the beginning, God created the heaven and the earth. . . .'

"Spontaneously performed, this humble testimony to faith was to millions the most moving moment of Apollo 8's drama-filled flight. To some, however, it seemed paradoxical that men reliant upon the most sophisticated instruments of science should at that moment feel the need to read the ancient words of the Bible. Such skeptics knew that in recent years it has been the fashion among certain scholars, scientists and historians to ridicule belief in the Bible, dismissing it as inexact historically, inaccurate scientifically, full of fables and myths.

"But today such cynicism seems curiously inappropriate. Consider: After 45 years of scholarly research, Robert Dick Wilson, former professor of Semitic philology at Princeton University, recently stated: 'I have come now to the conviction that no man knows enough to assail the truthfulness of the Old Testament. Where there is sufficient documentary evidence to make an investigation, the statements of the Bible in the original text have stood the test.'"

36 *How is God going to love me after what I've done this week? And I know I'll do it again! It doesn't make sense that He'll just forgive me over and over and over. I feel terribly guilty and just can't forgive myself for blowing it so bad — again!*

You're right. The natural reaction is to haul right off and smash you in the mouth!

Natural reaction

That's human. But, fortunately for all of us, that's not how God works. Man's reaction: slug you. God's reaction: love you.

Don't misunderstand. That's not to say God's a soft-touch grandpa who will let you climb all over Him and yank His beard and kick over His rocking chair. Some people look at God like that, [1] but actually, He's the virile God who made volcanoes as well as tulips. He can't stand sin, and He must judge it.

[1] See J. B. Phillips' *Your God Is Too Small.*

85

Yet He loves you in spite of your failures, because as He looks at you, He sees His Son Jesus. As you fail, you keep coming back to Him — confessing your sins — and He welcomes you.

That's not to say you're unconcerned. Your motivation in life is to please Jesus — to keep the fellowship close. First John 2:1 and 2 explains it this way: "I am telling you this so that you will stay away from sin. But if you sin, there is Someone to plead for you before the Father. His name is Jesus Christ, the one who is all that is good and who pleases God completely. He is the one who took God's wrath against our sins upon Himself, and brought us into fellowship with God. . . ."

You may have an image of your commitment to Christ making you some Joe Super Saint — super kind, always bubbling over with love, never ticked off. But you're human. God has entered your life, and He's changing it [2]

So — learn to forgive yourself when God does. If you don't, aren't you saying you know more than God?

[2] Still hassled? Read *Love Is Now*, by Peter Gillquist, (Zondervan).

TEMPTATION

Up
against
it

37 *I'm tempted to do all sorts of wrong things. I'm getting tired of fighting it, 'cause I keep doing what I know God gets mad at me for. Am I so terribly sinful that I have to be tempted like this all the time?*

Welcome to the Family! You're normal.

You can probably sympathize with the World War II sailor who originated the word "snafu." He was so frustrated one day that he signaled, "Situation Normal: All Fouled Up." The word quickly entered America's vocabulary.

Situation Normal: All Fouled Up. That's why Jesus had to come in the first place. And even after you've received Him into your life, you'll find temptations to go back to the old ways. Look at what First Corinthians 10:13 has to say: "But remember this — the wrong desires that come into your life aren't anything new and different. Many others have faced exactly the same problems before you. And no temptation is irresistible. You can trust God to keep the temptation from becoming so strong that you can't stand up against it, for He has promised this and will do what He says. He will show you how to escape temptation's power so that you can bear up patiently against it."

Your situation's normal: all fouled up. But God changes that. James 1:12-15 declares, "Happy is the man who doesn't give in and do wrong when he is tempted, for afterwards he will get as his reward the crown of life that God has promised those who love Him. And remember, when someone wants to do wrong it is never God who is tempting him, for God never wants to do wrong and never tempts anyone else to do it. Temptation is the pull of man's own evil thoughts and wishes. These evil thoughts lead to evil actions and afterwards to the death penalty from God."

So we can't simply relax and float downstream. We can't just give in. For when we see the seriousness of sin, we see how important it is to yield to Christ. Peter, perhaps more than anyone else, saw in a terrible, graphic scene just what his sin cost God. He denied Christ three times. Then he saw soldiers lead Jesus away to a whipping which ripped open His body, then a cruel execution by spikes through hands and feet. And Peter wept when he saw how he had failed God. Years later Peter said, "Obey God because you are His children; don't slip back into your old ways — doing evil because you knew no better. But be holy now in everything you do, just as the Lord is holy, who invited you to be His child." [1]

Our natural inclination is to drift from God. We want to give in. But God waits patiently for us to invite Him to take over inside us, to fight the battles that are bigger than we are.

[1] 1 Peter 1:14 and 15.

38 *Let me tell you about the real me. I tell lies about other people. I lust after girls. I'm self-centered, and I put other people down. In fact, I enjoy putting them down. What do you say to that?*

Your comments are very similar to others we keep hearing. For instance:

"I'm terribly jealous, and I can't help myself."

"I resent people who hurt me — I just about hate them!"

"All I want to do is escape and do what feels good all the time."

"I can't stand my sister, and sometimes I think I'm going to kill her."

It should be no surprise that the old self in you produces some alarmingly evil things. The surprise is, God has a remedy. We confess our sins, reject them from our lives, and God forgives us and moves in to control.

Here are some tips:

• Remember that you're a son or daughter of God, even when you're hassling.

• Stay away from things that trip you up. If lust is a problem, reading *Playboy* or *Penthouse* is not going to help. If friends drag you down, search for some who will lift you up.

• It's not bad to cry "help" if you need it—from other kids, your Sunday School teacher, church youth leader, a pastor—anyone who can talk and pray and encourage you.

• Accept God's forgiveness as a prod to victory. Psalm 37:23 and 24 says, "The steps of good men are directed by the Lord. He delights in each step they take. If they fall, it isn't fatal, for the Lord holds them with His hand."

39 *How do I know what Satan's thoughts are and what God's are? Does Satan really get involved in what I do every day?*

Jesus referred to Satan quite a bit. He called him the prince of the power of the air. It's rather shocking that Jesus didn't contradict this evil prince when he claimed that he — Satan — could hand over earth's kingdoms to Jesus. Apparently the devil controls quite a lot on this planet!

However, Jesus also said he saw Satan fall like a shooting star from heaven.[1] Christ smashed him, defeated his power through His death on the cross. And we now share Christ's victory!

Unfortunately, you can get into some unhealthy scenes if you make a fetish about thinking of Satan all the time and see him or his demons haunting your bedroom or stirring around in your soup. The best

Demons
in
the soup?

[1] Luke 10:18-20.

advice is to stay as far away from him and the occult as you can. [2]

But Satan is real, and you should be aware of his plans for you.

You now have two major reasons for *new* conflict in your life. *One:* Before you became a Christian, you had just one set of impulses — basically selfish — with a watered-down conscience tagging along. Now, you have God's new impulses in you, and these war against each other. [3] *Two:* You've taken on a new enemy. You're now a threat to Satan. Before, he was relatively happy with you because you were going his way. You were part of his family. Now, you have a new Father: you're part of God's family, and your Father's enemy is your enemy. Satan is unhappy to have lost you, and the least he can do now is work you over. And here's his battle plan:

Doubt. Satan will try to immobilize you by making you think that perhaps all this Bible and Jesus business is just a hopeful theory anyway, and that you can't be sure, so why be so serious about it?

Discouragement. Satan tries to make you look at your problems instead of the Problem-Solver. Jesus once invited Peter to walk on the lake. [4] And as Peter looked at Jesus, he started doing it. Peter was actually walking on water! But as soon as he started worrying about being right in the middle of the lake and how wet he'd be if this miracle stopped, *and he took his eyes off Jesus,* kersplash! Down he went. And Jesus had to reach out and drag him back to the boat.

Diversion. Satan will be sure to make this very attractive. Something you want more than anything else. A boyfriend or girlfriend. A car. A grade on a test. But it will be a dead-end street, a counterfeit of the enriching things God wants you to have.

[2] James 4:1-8; 1 Peter 5:8-11.
[3] See Romans 7:15-26.
[4] Matthew 14:22-33.

Failure. We all know how it feels
to lose, get shoved aside. So what
answers does God have, now that you're
linked up with Him?

Defeat. Satan will make you feel, "Well, I really blew it. Guess I'm just not cut out to be a Christian. Might as well fail again since I failed these other times." Satan wants to convert your one failure into many. He majors on our past mistakes, whereas God majors on the future and what we are becoming. God forgives. The devil reminds you of your worst failures. The Apostle Paul was very realistic about this. He says in Philippians 3:13 and 14, "No, dear brothers, I am still not all I should be but I am bringing all my energies to bear on this one thing: Forgetting the past and looking forward to what lies ahead, I strain to reach the end of the race and receive the prize for which God is calling us up to heaven because of what Christ Jesus did for us."

Delay. Why should Satan bother to talk you out of something when he can just get you to postpone it? It's like that diet you're going to start tomorrow. Always *tomorrow!* If he can get you to put off doing what you know Christ wants you to, he'll have you sliding his way.

James 4:7 tells us: "So give yourselves humbly to God. Resist the devil and he will flee from you."

Let each conflict make you more like Jesus, because you include Him in the battle.

All of Satan's attacks will be based on one thing: a lie. Jesus said this about the devil: "He was a murderer from the beginning and a hater of truth — there is not an iota of truth in him. When he lies, it is perfectly normal; for he is the father of liars." [5]

Be encouraged, for you have Truth on your side. No matter how great the hangup, Jesus has been in there and licked it. Jesus tells us, "Here on earth you will have many trials and sorrows; but cheer up, for I have overcome the world." [6]

[5] John 8:44.
[6] John 16:33.

40 *My girlfriend is falling away from God. How can I reach her without her rejecting me?*

It's possible you can't.

We hear a lot of similar questions. Unfortunately, often a guy and a gal may be going opposite directions, one with God and the other away from Him. And that hurts when you really care for each other.

In today's world, the music you listen to and films and books constantly tell you love's the one thing that makes life worth living. "Can't do without you," comes softly to your ears. "Without you, Babe, I'll be lost," rocks into your car. So, many kids figure the most important thing in the world is keeping the relationship they've got — or going out to find one.

Love between a girl and boy is a beautiful thing. God meant it to be, and He's all for it. But allowing God to take charge of your life is even more important. When you find you have to change too much to keep someone — when you have to shove God into a corner — it's time to say the relationship takes second place.[1]

Yes, it would be nice if you could reach her without her rejecting you. Let's hope you can. Live Christ-like, showing the fruits of the Spirit.[2] Pray. Ask God to show you His plan. But don't delude yourself. It may be that God will force you to make a choice — perhaps the hardest one yet.

[1] 2 Corinthians 6:14-18.
[2] Galatians 5:22 and 23.

"Without you, Babe . . ."

41 *Maybe God put my parents in charge of me, but He sure picked a couple of losers. The only God in my home is a "god-damn." I fight with my mom all the time, and I'm barely on speaking terms with my dad. They don't understand anything about where I'm coming from.*

Perhaps your parents really are at fault most of the time. But perhaps it's also true that you don't understand where they're coming from either.

But let's say God has put you into a battleground. That your parents are tyrants and grouches. That you're a victim. The worst they can be is enemies. Downright nasty, they're-out-to-get-me-type enemies.

But Jesus said we have to love our enemies.

So, the question is, how in the world do you get the strength to love *them*? Well, you can't. That's the whole point. All you can do is open yourself up to Christ. Ask Him to pour in *His* love and change your attitudes even if you are right and they're totally wrong.

No, it's not easy. In fact, it's impossible! Only Jesus Christ can do the impossible in you.

We're not, of course, only talking about warm emotions of love. No, Jesus calls for your *specific* acts. "A soft answer turns away wrath." [1] "Turn the other cheek." [2] Scriptures like that give you principles. It's up to you to list specific actions.

For some real down-to-earth help, read the book of James and the Gospel of John, chapters 14 - 17. Then read Proverbs.

[1] Proverbs 15:1 and 2.
[2] Matthew 5:39.

Home, sweet home

42 *When I'm with my boyfriend, sometimes I think and want to do lustful things—like standing too close and other stuff. How can I stop thinking that way?*

There is such a thing as lust, and you may be going too far with your boyfriend. But don't try to make yourself sexless. You were made to have sexual thoughts — you're a sexual being.

God made something very beautiful when He made sex. He knows all about how you feel and think sexually, because He created sex — for you. And His aim is for you to have the most pleasure and true joy possible, with commitments which protect and enrich the whole person.

That's why He set up marriage.

But that's not to say you're not a sexual person now. A touch, a kiss, a hug — all expressions and thoughts about sex depend on your level of commitment to the other person and how God is working in you.

Bring your sex life and thoughts to the Lord, and ask Him for His guidance and understanding. In our sex-saturated society, most of us have to fight its becoming an obsession. But again, it's your opportunity to invite Christ into a specific area. [1]

Accept your sexuality. Accept Christ's control over it.

[1] 1 Corinthians 6:18-20.

43 *I received Christ a few weeks ago. But I'm confused about what I really am. Some of my friends and teachers think the whole idea of sin and rules and a religion that says it knows the truth is silly. They say all these ideas developed years ago to fit the times, and that we have to develop our own ideas now and shake off old superstitions.*

It's true that many people look around, don't see God on a cloud or walking down streets and figure man is just one more uneasy rider on planet Earth. As he spins around on it like monkeys and snails, he's smarter — but not really different.

This reasoning is common, and it's easy to see where it comes from. You've probably taken a biology course in which you study the life cycle. A cute little rabbit is born; he grows up eating clover and Mr. MacGregor's lettuce, and after awhile, he dies, and his body mixes with the earth. This helps new clover to grow so more bunnies can eat clover to then die to fertilize more clover to feed more bunnies. Water and earth, rabbits and clover, man and hot dogs — all are part of the cycle of life and death, going on year after year after year.

And that's all there is!

But can you believe you're simply a fancy fertilizer? Are you no more than burgers and french fries and soon just food for geraniums? After death — nothing? Nothing at all?

Deep within, people have always known there is more. You've always known it. The Bible says we know God from just looking around at what He's made. [1]

Jesus knows. In the Gospels, you find Him often talking about judgment and afterlife. [2] The Bible

[1] See Romans, the first three chapters.
[2] John 5:19-29, for example.

99

You can find intelligent people believing
almost anything. So how can a person sift
through the conflicting ideas and find
Truth?

clearly indicates, Yes, you will be alive a hundred years from now! Probably not in an old folks' home. Between now and then some auto accident or cancer or war or just plain tired blood will have gotten you. (Or, Jesus may have returned.) But you *will* be alive! Thinking. Doing. Feeling. Either with God, or separated from Him.

We can't live like rabbits

If that's true, we can't live like mere rabbits. We're more than fertilizer for grass on our nicely mown graves. We will live for thousands of years — think of that! — and our life-style now must be caught up into God, for we're only beginning a million years of Life!

Of course, anyone can choose to disbelieve all this. That is the choice. That is the crucial decision each person must make. But to put it all down, a person must decide against what God is telling him by His creation and His Word — and to disregard the way morally-diseased humans act, obviously worse than rabbits. Evil stalks us, embedded in man, and it, too, is proof that we are ultimately more than fertilizer.

44 *Can you tell me what's going on? I mean, everything's falling apart! Every time I pick up a newspaper I read about somebody getting shot, or a jet crashing and killing hundreds of people, or an earthquake leveling whole towns. Even when I can look out the window and see a beautiful day, I think about all the people who are starving and dying. You get to the point where you can't enjoy anything anymore, because somebody's being murdered or divorced or discriminated against or something.*

Many of us feel the same emotions about the world situation as you do—as we hear of new, horrible things that happen to people or that people do to each other.

Seeing earth through God's eyes

To understand all this, we have to see the world from God's eyes. How does *He* view the murdered people lying in the streets or the homeless or the starving? Actually, He knows facts we are quick to forget.

The world is condemned.

Perhaps you've seen an old house or building with a condemned sign on its paint-blistered front door. Broken floors. Rafters hanging down. Dangerous. The house is not at all what it originally was meant to be. It's marked for destruction.

Perhaps also you've seen photos of men who are condemned, chained and led off away from free citizens. Led off to eventual death.

Most of us would rather not think about such scenes, but God says that's just the way the world is. Condemned. Like a man on death row. John 3:17 says, "God did not send His Son into the world to condemn it, but to save it."

The world was already condemned. Jesus came because it was condemned. And it still is (have you noticed it's not getting any better?). The world is made up of people, and the ugly fact is that humans are condemned. We are a race of doomed creatures.

The Bible is very clear on this:

"The heart is deceitful above all things, and desperately wicked: who can know it?" [1]

"Yes, all have sinned; all fall short of God's glorious ideal. . . ." [2]

But the Bible also gives a solution:

"For the wages of sin is death, but the free gift of God is eternal life through Jesus Christ our Lord." [3]

God originally made man "in His own image." He made him to do good and to love others. He also made him to have the highest destiny of all God's created beings. Man was to be an honor and glory to his Maker.

God also made people significant. They weren't just cows in a field. They could choose God's way or evil.

[1] Jeremiah 17:9.
[2] Romans 3:23.
[3] Romans 6:32.

Unfortunately, they chose evil. They chose selfishness, instead of God.

And that's why people are such an incredible mixture. People are great, but contaminated. They are like the prized possessions of thousands of recent flood victims. Families watched sewer waters contaminate their books, chairs, carpets, stereos, radios and very personal items. They eventually pitched these precious, excellent things into the street for a garbage pickup. Good for nothing, yet originally of high value. And in the same way that people looked at their goods in the streets and felt terrible about their loss, God looked at His contaminated creation — man, turned rebel — and wept. And He sent His Son to reclaim His creation.

Care for orphans; cheat the poor

Men and women can write brilliant books, care for orphans, develop moon rockets, create music and art of high genius — but they also cheat the poor and murder Olympians. Man is great. God made him that way. But he is also fallen, and his great achievements are soaked in sourness, because God has been — for the most part — ignored.

That's why Jesus came. To "save the world," one person at a time. To graft in a whole new life. To pump in new blood, new goals, a new allegiance. [4]

A condemned building is good for nothing but destruction — unless somebody *completely* renovates it. New beams. New floors. New roof. New doors. And that's how complete the job is which Jesus proposes to do in you. It's begun when you received Him. You were made new right then. But Jesus still has a lot of carpentry to do as He brings you to maturity and teaches you just what His perfection is all about. For He plans to make you just like Himself.

A condemned man is led away to death row — unless the President offers him a pardon. If he does, the President is saying, "You are guilty. That has been proven in a court of law. But the state forgives you. You are free." This is exactly what Jesus says to us. We were condemned to death. Not some light punishment. Death. We were guilty. But the Father has pardoned us — because Jesus was executed and carried our sins with Him to the town garbage dump where He was strung up and painfully murdered.

A prisoner in 1830 named George Wilson was pardoned by the President. They brought Wilson the pardon, but he refused to accept it because it would mean admitting his guilt. So he walked to the hangman's noose with the pardon in his pocket.

That's what each human is like. We have pardons in our pockets. But most people ignore their guilt, ignore the pardon, the new life, the love and power He offers. So the murders and hatreds go on.

[4] See Romans 3:9-26.

45 *Why did Jesus have to die? I can understand our need to be forgiven — that's obvious. But why did He have to be tortured to death just so God could set us free? If God is almighty, why couldn't He simply declare we're free and make it so? Isn't saying I'm sorry enough?*

Your question is like asking, "Why can't we fly with our arms?" or "Why can't we feed all the hungry of the world by thinking?'" Because that's not the way things are.

God is God. And He says in the Bible that the nature of things demands that innocent blood be

Why not fly with your arms?

spilled! In the Old Testament you'll read of lambs being killed to symbolically atone for Israeli sins and to foreshadow Jesus' atoning death. [1]

Perhaps it would help to think of a kid who steals $10 from his dad's wallet, spends it, then confesses. His dad may forgive, but the $10 now has to come from some place. And the kid can't pay it back. That's the way we are — no assets large enough to pay back our rebellion. [2]

But our human reasoning is not God's, so there's no further clear answer to be given. Except, perhaps, to say that the incredible seriousness of our crimes against God are seen clearly only when we understand that God Himself had to come to us and be executed — by us — for our sins against Him. If God were simply to say, "Everybody line up and say you're sorry. Okay, now everything's fine again!" — what sort of a God might He be?

[1] Leviticus 17:11.

[2] We are saved through grace by faith. (Eph. 2:8) Grace is God making up the difference between what I am without God and what I should be. Faith is saying yes to what He did.

Darkness crowds us. But how many
people are walking away from the light
into cold barrenness, ignoring that
which could enrich them and call
them to celebrate?

46 *I still have trouble believing in a final judgment and hell and all that. It doesn't make sense that so many people are going to be forever lost. Most of them have never heard about Jesus. What He really stood for, that is.*

One thing we know about God: He is fair. We don't know precisely how everything will turn out beyond this life, but we do know a holy and just God is in charge.

We also know the human race stands condemned — which is consternating, but true. We have to face facts.

It's strange that many people find it easy to accept the idea of heaven — fleecy clouds and meadows and streets of gold and lions lying down with lambs and everyone delighted forever — but reject the idea of hell. Both places come from the same Bible.

Just because people ignore something doesn't mean it isn't there.

When Jewish prisoners sat in Auschwitz and Buchenwald during World War II, they would watch the smoke rise out of the stacks of the crematoriums and wonder what it meant. Some thought they were giant boilers heating water so they could finally take nice, warm showers. Others said they were making soap, although they never saw any. No one admitted what some must have suspected. These people marched quietly, 3,000 at a time, into enormous "shower rooms," supposedly to be disinfected. The rooms did not look like death chambers until the prisoners saw that the soap was actually stone and the shower heads fake. Many had previously watched thousands of their friends go to their deaths, but they ignored the facts.

Unlike the Auschwitz Jews, we have "a way of escape" — Jesus Christ.

In the same way, people don't want to talk about judgment and hell. Not in our "enlightened" society. However, though we don't know precisely what hell will be like, we know God judges men. The Bible says man's punishment is to be separated from God forever. [1]

How can this be?

In one sense, God is not going to judge us—we judge ourselves. Read the first few chapters of Romans. Every person—Indochinese, South African, or American knows a basic right and wrong. Every person has a standard of his own. It may be twisted from God's perfect standard, but it's a moral code. The judgment is this: no man anywhere has ever lived up to his own moral code. We keep violating our own standards. And in the day of judgment, the question will be, "Did you live up to the light God gave you?" (True, some men, like the Marquis de Sade, reject nearly all of God's light and therefore reject Him. But that in itself is obvious judgment.)

Many would criticize us for writing this sort of thing. Unhealthy. Medieval myth. Scare-mongering. But that's like saying it's not polite to talk about what happened at the Munich Olympics. That Buchenwald should never be thought of. That we have problems, but they aren't so bad.

Our problems are so bad that Jesus — the only truly good Man who ever lived — had to be executed for them.

He now offers new life — and a new destiny — to anyone who will reject his sins, believe in Him and invite Him to do radical things in his life.

[1] 2 Thessalonians 1:5-10.

47 *I don't particularly think all this talk about my being so sinful is healthy — is it? Okay, maybe I am a louse. But I have enough problems now believing in myself. Where's it going to get me to tell myself I'm crummy all the time? I might as well go stick my head in a concrete mixer right now if I'm going to keep saying that Jesus is wonderful, but I'm no good.*

Self-honesty is the best road to health.

The fact that you see yourself as infected with a fatal moral disease — that you are a selfish creature — is not psychological suicide. It is the means to wholeness. Look around and you see the selfishness of man. Look inside, and you sense something terribly wrong. To ignore all this is like ignoring cancer.

Something wrong inside

But looking within, you also see the incredibly high potential you have. You see the true self God wants

111

to restore. Your "goodness" is now irrelevant. You have a new life in Christ, and you live in *His* goodness.

You are unique. A person in the deepest sense. A marvelous creation of God. He has given you new life, and a new self.

Under no conditions go about hating yourself. That's not the idea at all. You're right in saying that approach would be terribly unhealthy. Jesus said, "Love

I'm OK. Are you?

your neighbor as much as you love yourself." [1] Included in His statement is the factor of loving yourself. You accept a growing appreciation for yourself, as it is linked with God. You are therefore becoming what God originally intended you to be.

But you can't do this on your own. Warfare rages inside. Your old self clashes against the new. Expect conflict. Expect the battles to result in His victory in you. For God's plan in this world is to draw out of it a community of people who will love Him forever — and, because you've personally received Him, you're one of them!

[1] Matthew 22:34-40.

112

God's plan is to draw out a community
of people who love Him—
and you're one of them!

What Jesus Said About Himself . . .

I am the One who raises the dead
and gives them life again. Anyone who
believes in Me, even though he dies
like anyone else, shall live again.

                    I am the light of the world.

I have been given all authority
in heaven and earth.

            I was in existence before
            Abraham was ever born!

            The world's sin is unbelief in Me.

I am the Way — yes,
the Truth and the Life.
No one can get to the Father
except by means of Me.

                I am the Bread of Life. No one
            coming to Me will ever be hungry again.
            Those believing in Me will never thirst.

My purpose is to give
eternal life — abundantly.

                    If you trust Me, you
                    are really trusting God.

            I am the Good Shepherd.
        The Good Shepherd lays down
            His Life for the sheep.

Read the Gospel of John, Chapters 14 - 18 for more direct
statements from Jesus.

So — what does God expect, now that He's done so much for you? Like the sign on the highway says — "yield." God now has the right-of-way in your life. Which means that not only will you have fewer smash-ups, but you'll be traveling down His highway in His Way, with the power He provides. Life genuinely becomes an adventure.

But it's not all blue sky. In a sense, God "never promised you a rose garden." You live in a world corrupted by evil, and getting onto God's side puts you right at the heart of the battle. Expect struggle and rough going — but also expect growth and victory, because He's in charge of you from here on out.